# Akello Akunda Gukora Iki?

What does Akello love to do?

Written by Dr. Sarah Eyaa
Translated by Mr. Patrick Ineza
Illustrated by TitanSign

First Published 2022
Copyright © Sarah Eyaa

Translator: Patrick Ineza
Illustrator: Titan Sign

All Rights Reserved. No part of this book may be reproduced, distributed, stored in a retrieval system, or transmitted in any form or by any means without the prior written permission of the author, except in the case of brief quotations embodied in critical reviews and certain other noncommercial uses permitted by copyright law.

ISBN - 978-0-6454427-3-1

# Dedication

This book is dedicated to my family and all people who are seeking to learn a local language.

# Acknowledgement

I would like to thank Ms. Maureen Kananura for proofreading this book.

This book belongs to

_____

_____

# Suhuza Akello

Akello numukobwa muto wo mubwoko bwa Lango. Ubu bwoko bukomoka mu Majyaruguru ya Uganda kandi buvuga ururimi ruzwi nka Leb-Lango. Iki gitabo kitwereka ibintu Akello akunda gukora.

# Meet Akello

Akello is a little girl from the Lango tribe. This tribe comes from Northern Uganda and speaks a language known as Leb-Lango. This book shows us the things that Akello loves doing.

Akello akunda gukina na musaza we Obua
(Akello loves playing with her brother Obua)

Akello akunda gusoma ibitabo
(Akello loves reading books)

**Akello akunda gushushanya**
(Akello loves drawing)

Akello akunda kujya ku isoko hamwe na nyina
(Akello loves going to the market with her mother)

Akello akunda kurira ibiti
(Akello loves climbing trees)

Akello akunda kumwenyura
(Akello loves smiling)

Ukunda gukora iki? Ndizera ko wakunze gusoma ibijyanye nibyo Akello akunda gukora.

(What do you love to do? I hope you enjoyed reading about what Akello loves to do.)

*The End*

www.ingramcontent.com/pod-product-compliance
Lightning Source LLC
Chambersburg PA
CBHW041428010526
44107CB00045B/1536